How to Start Making Money Online

Colvin Tonya Nyakundi

Entrepreneur Book Series

Mendon Cottage Books

JD-Biz Publishing

Check out some of the other Entrepreneur Series books
Entrepreneur Series books on Amazon
Check out some of the Science of Living Series books
Science of Living Series on Amazon
Check out some of the Health Learning Series books
Health Learning Series on Amazon

Table of Contents

Introduction

The internet has totally revolutionized how people do business. Unlike in the past where employers and employees had to be in constant physical contact, currently you can employ somebody who is thousands of miles away. Actually, it is now normal to hear of a large company whose employees are distributed over different countries or continents. The demand for online workforce is ever increasing due to the increase in internet penetration in different parts of the world. This means that there are currently unlimited jobs that you can do over the internet from any part of the world

One major advantage of freelancing through the internet is that you get to be your own boss. This means that you'll be the one managing your time and deciding the nature of job you want to do. You also have the freedom to choose when and where to do your job as long as you meet your clients' specifications.

With experience and dedication to your job, the internet can pay very well. This is part of the reason as to why more and more people are leaving their permanent jobs so as to establish their presence on the internet and start doing online jobs.

Apart from the fact that you get to interact with several people from different parts of the world, the internet also provides a platform for you to display your skills and experience(s) to a larger population. This means that you are likely to have a larger customer base over the internet than anywhere else.

With this and many more advantages of doing online jobs, anybody who's interested in making extra cash can't afford to ignore reading the book "How to Start Making Money online". This book is designed to help anybody thinking of doing online jobs. Even if you have experience in doing online jobs, you still need to read this book so as to learn how you can expand your online resume and hence increase your income.

Inside this book you'll find tips on how to relate with your assistants and clients so as to grow your business (online company.) By simply reading the book "How to

Start Making Money Online," you'll learn skills on how to secure your online business by avoiding cyber criminals and conmen.

If you're a newcomer in doing online jobs, all you need to do is read this book and you'll get a list of all jobs that you can do over the internet.

Start your journey to a secure and financially stable future by reading "How to Start Making Money Online!!!"

Where to Make Money Online

There are so many avenues that amateur and experienced freelancers can use to start making money over the internet. However, it is highly advisable that you stick to the kind of jobs that you have passion in or are talented in. With passion and talent, you'll always do high quality jobs and meet your clients' needs with minimal setbacks. This means that you'll find it quite easy to grow your resume and start making huge sums of money. Here is a list of jobs you can do over the internet:

Blogging

By definition, a blog is a platform on the internet where someone can share his/her hobbies and experiences each day. Whereas there are millions of private blogs, there are also those run for commercial purposes. If you have a large audience on your blog, you can make money by selling advertisement space to merchants. You can also make cash through blogs by writing content for other people. Remember that some people will do anything to make sure that they have several subscribers to their online blogs. This means that they're always willing to pay good cash to anybody willing to write content that can attract many visitors. Large and small companies may also hire you to interact with their clients through their official blogs. If you're thinking of how to start making money over the internet, then you need to consider blogging.

Creating websites and search engine optimization

In the current world, no company can dare claim that it is well established if it doesn't have an online presence. Even for those companies with online presence, they still need to be ranked highly by search engines such as Google. The demand for website developers and search engine optimization experts is very high and therefore more companies are willing to splash huge sums of cash to anybody who can help them establish a highly ranked website. If you have experience in creating websites, this is your opportunity to start making cash by creating websites for companies and other people in any part of the world. You can also make significant amounts of cash if you have skills in search engine optimization. There are several websites that offer a platform for website developers and search engine optimization experts to meet potential clients and start doing business.

Affiliate marketing

With more and more companies planning to expand their presence to new areas, there is always constant demand for advertisers. If you're running a website on any particular niche, you can rest assured that there is a company somewhere willing to allow you advertise their products on their behalf. This is what is referred to as affiliate marketing. There are two ways in which you can make money through affiliate marketing. In the first way, you place the adverts on your website and then get paid on a per click basis –you agree with the merchant on the amount of cash you'll be paid if somebody clicks on an advert on your website before being redirected to the merchant's website. Generally, you won't be paid a lot of money this way because not all the people who click on an advert will purchase the merchants products. In the second way, you get paid on a per acquisitions basis i.e. you're only paid when somebody purchase products on the merchants website after being redirected from your website. The second way generally pays more cash than the first way. Affiliate marketing is one of the best ways to start making money online especially if you have high traffic on your website. However, you need to be very careful when placing advertisements so as not to be a spammer. Remember that your website's subscribers might avoid your website if they feel like there is too much unnecessary stuff (spam).

Data entry

Data entry is one of the simplest and easiest jobs that you can ever do over the internet. Unlike other jobs that may require one to do some research, data entry doesn't need any form of research. All that is required is for you to be very accurate and fast in data entry. You can be given a scanned document (in PDF or jpeg format) and then asked to write it in word document.

Writing e-books

Before the internet became popular, one had to do research by visiting a library or conducting face to face interviews. However, nowadays more and more people tend to search for answers over the internet. This means that there are so many people willing to buy e-books pertaining to their topic of research. There are also those who prefer buying softcopies of novels instead of hardcopies. This means that they're willing to invest their cash on some of the highly ranked novels available online. If you're thinking of making some extra cash, then you might want to start writing e-books. You can do this by doing some research on the most interesting or highly searched topics. You'll then go ahead and write an e-book before publishing it and making it available on merchant websites such as Amazon. If you're very good at writing e-books, you can also be contracted by somebody else to write an e-book on their behalf.

Selling your products online

Are you an aspiring musician or entrepreneur? If yes, then you might want to kick-start your career through the internet. For example, you can sing a song at home and then place it on YouTube®. If you're a talented singer/songstress, a good record label might sign you and soon you'll be making more cash than you could have ever imagined. After you've become an established musician, you can still use the internet to market your music. If you've just opened a retail store, then you might want to increase your customer numbers by marketing your products online. You can then go ahead and deliver your products to customers on their doorsteps. You can sell all types of commodities including electronics, toys, furniture, packed meals etc.

Computer programming

Are you a professional computer programmer or do you have skills and experience in programming languages such as java, C++ or python? Rather than just sitting and waiting to get a job somewhere else, you might want to start freelancing. As a matter of fact, the demand for computer programmers is so high that you can never miss a job if you're keen on getting one. There are so many websites and companies willing to instantly hire experienced computer programmers. All you have to do is identify one of them and then you'll start making money soon.

Testing games and mobile applications

The process of developing mobile phone and computer games and applications involves several stages that may take several weeks or even months. Even after a game or an application has been developed, it is possible that it might be having several bugs and errors. So as to minimize the probability of having errors, game and application developers hire other people to test the apps and/or games. For instance, you can be hired to play a given game several times the whole day just to make sure that it doesn't crash your system or hang your computer. Due to the simple and easy way of doing this job, anybody can do it as long as they know how to use a computer. However, the net pay in such jobs is generally low and hence you should do them if you have nothing else to do.

- Increasing traffic and activity in other people's website.

Even though this job has lower returns when compared to other online jobs, you might want to do it since it is so simple and easy. All that you'll be doing is going through the content posted on your client's blog or website and then comment regularly. This way, your employer's website will increase its ranking due to increased traffic.

Transcribing

Transcribing is basically listening to a given video or audio clip and then writing down what you hear. This job is very simple as the only thing required is for you to be conversant with the language being spoken in the clip. Transcribing is also related to video and audio editing jobs. If you know how to create special effects on video or audio clips, you might want to try using your skills to make some extra cash.

Translation

Translation jobs are also becoming more and more popular as people from different parts of the world try to interact with each other. Even after an application or game has been developed, the developer might want to translate the original user language into several languages. This means that you can make cash if you're fluent in several highly spoken languages.

Designing logos

Throughout the world, thousands or even tens of thousands of new companies and enterprises are incorporated each year. They're looking for unique and highly noticeable logos. Some of these companies are willing to invest huge amounts of cash in logo design just to make sure that they have a logo that clearly distinguishes their brands and places them on top of their competitors. If you're very creative and have skills in logo design, you might want to exploit your skills to make some extra cash.

Taking part in research and surveys

A few decades ago, the only way that one could conduct survey was by interviewing respondents face to face. However, over the past decade research firms have totally shifted from conducting face to face interviews to online interviews. Apart from the high number of participants likely to take part in online surveys, it also takes very little time and the researcher is likely to get more accurate information as respondents are guaranteed of their confidentiality. This is why research firms are always willing to give incentives to anybody willing to take part in their research. You can therefore make some extra cash by being one of the respondents in an online survey.

- Buying and selling domains

The business of buying and selling domains is also one of the ways you can make easy and quick cash over the internet. It is on record that a multinational company spent more than $200,000 in acquisition of a domain whose initials rhymed with the company's initials. In this kind of job, all you have to do is look at trending topics and then buy a domain likely to fetch more money once you sell it.

Online jobs are not only limited to those listed above. You can also do any other job that requires one to do it on a computer and then submit it in soft copy. This means that you should always be on the lookout for new opportunities to start making cash online.

Online Communication with Clients and Assistants

When compared to other workplaces, the internet is very different as you might never meet your clients or even assistants (employees). You might also be working as a group with a bunch of people from different geographical regions while you've never met them and don't have an idea as to how they look like. This therefore means that the nature of communication between you and your assistants and clients might be a little complex because you probably don't know them. In spite of the large distance between you and your clients and assistants you should never be tempted to ignore the importance of nurturing good communication habits with them. The only way you can advance your online career is by knowing how to communicate with your clients and assistants.

The first thing that you need to be wary of is the first impression you create after meeting a client or assistant (online) for the first time. First impression is not only good for the real world but also in online platforms as people will have a rough idea of your personality from the way you engage with them for the first few minutes or hours. After chatting or video conferencing with your potential clients or assistants for a few minutes, they'll have an idea of what to expect from you. This means that you ought to be very careful about your first impression.

Forming a trustworthy and reliable relationship with your clients and assistants is also one of the most important things when doing online jobs. Even if you're not in physical contact with them, you shouldn't give them any reason to doubt your ability to fulfill your promises. In other words, you have to be a man of your own words; if you promise to do something, you have to work hard to make sure that you do it so as not to disappoint your clients or assistants.

When doing online jobs, you have to be respectful to all your clients and assistants regardless of their current geographical location, religion, race, skin color or even body size. Without respecting them, nobody will be willing to do business with you after the first encounter. This means that it will be very difficult to grow your online business as you'll keep on changing your assistants now and then.

You should also ensure that you respond to your client's questions and concerns exhaustively and in time. Without this important communication ability, your business will be destined for doom. You should also ensure that you have all the facts before responding to any of the queries raised by your clients. This means that you must never be in a hurry to answer a question without doing some research and figuring out what you're required to do.

Giving clear and precise instructions is also one of the most important communication techniques for all those doing online jobs. Without giving clear instructions, your assistants might end up doing something totally different from what you expected. It will therefore be a total waste of their time, energy and resources. If you frequently give vague, ambiguous and contradicting instructions, you might end up losing your entire workforce to other more organized people.

As part of improving the communication between you and your assistants, you should always try to motivate them as much as possible. You can do this by for example giving them occasional bonuses or making their work easier by recommending sources of information for certain tasks. With motivation, your online business will grow significantly as more and more people will be willing to come and work for you. You can also motivate your clients in so many ways. For example, you can slash the money you charge them. This way more and more people will be willing to hire you as soon as they have a job you're qualified to do.

You can also improve your communication skills by making sure that you're always online or you frequently refresh your electronic mail box. Nothing feels as disappointing as having to wait for several hours before an assistant or client can get back to you. This means that the only way you can maintain your clientele and even attract more customers is by making sure that you're always online.

You also need to keep a digital directory/diary of all your obligations, assignments and employee tasks. This will help you to properly manage your time and know when you're expected to talk to your clients and assistants. Without a digital diary, you'll find it quite challenging to communicate with your clients and assistants.

Regardless of the nature of online job you do, you must never forget the importance of honesty to your clients and assistants. Even if it looks like things will get worse if you tell the truth, in the long run it will be more advantageous to tell the truth than lie.

How to Grow Your Online Resume

It is everybody's dream to grow their careers as much as possible. Most people will therefore do anything as long as they advance in their careers. There are certain aspects of life that you need to learn about if you're keen on growing your online resume. Always keep in mind that nothing comes easily in life. It is therefore up to you to strive hard in all your online jobs so as to grow your resume. Here are some of the ways in which you can grow your online resume:

- Commitment

After you've been allocated a given task by your client, you must strive to ensure that you do it. Commitment is all about doing everything in your power to make sure that you don't disappoint your clients. Without this simple but important rule (commitment), there is no way you can advance in your online career. Commitment involves investing your energy, time and resources to make sure that you deliver what your clients are expecting. Remember that you can never sow where you did not plant. The only way you can sow (grow your career) is by planting something (investing your time, energy and resources.)

- Deliver high quality results

You should never compromise the quality of the assignments that you've been allocated by your clients. Since most online jobs involve doing research on the internet and then coming up with unique content, some people might be tempted to plagiarize their work or even give data/information from unreliable sources. If you're keen on growing your online resume, you must always ensure that you deliver accurate, well researched and unique assignments.

- Do your job instead of giving excuses

In life, you might have come across people who like giving so many excuses instead of doing the job they've been allocated. If you have this kind of behavior, you should try to improve on it as you won't ever grow your career. As a matter of fact, nobody will dare hire you again if you disappointed them the first time.

- Be distinguishable from all the others

Being distinguishable entails offering services or products that cannot be matched by your competitors. This important trait also entails offering high quality services and products to all your clients. By simply being distinguishable from all your competitors you can grow your online resume to levels that you could never have imagined before.

- Be updated on emerging trends

The internet is a very dynamic place and new products and services keep on being launched each day. This means that the only way you can grow your online resume is by adjusting to the new trends. You should make sure that you adjust to new and emerging trends among different groups of people.

- Create an online profile and showcase your resume

Most clients are looking for a freelancer who is not only skilled but also qualified for the job. This means that you have a higher chance of being hired if you make yourself known to potential clients by making your resume available to everybody. Try creating a profile on popular resume sites such as LinkedIn. You should also ensure that your resume is updated as soon as you achieve something new.

- Take advantage of the social media to advertise your services

Social networking websites offer the perfect platform for anybody to advertise their services. Currently, billions of people are active users in social networking sites such as Facebook, Twitter and Whatsapp. You can therefore take advantage of the high number of people to make sure that as many people as possible know about the kind of services you offer.

- Backup all your files

Even the most technologically advanced institutions are not one hundred percent secure from data corruption or loss. If you're keen on growing your online resume, you have to always ensure that you have a backup of all files stored in a different drive on an offline server. This way you can be sure that you won't ever fail to meet your obligations due to data loss or corruption.

- Adapt to new working conditions

When doing online jobs, you might be required to do different types of jobs from what you're experienced in. This means that the only way you can do such jobs is by learning how to adapt to new types of jobs and new environments.

- Take advantage of your talents

You can also grow your resume by simply, taking advantage of your talents to do a superb job. Remember that you're likely to perform better in something you're talented in than in something else.

- Collecting feedback and improving on your weaknesses

So as to grow your online resume, you should ensure that you collect feedback from your clients and improve on your weaknesses. By working on your weaknesses, you can offer your clients exactly what they're expecting from you.

How to Avoid Cyber Criminals

Try searching the internet for 'how to start making money online' and you'll be surprised at the millions of results that will be displayed within microseconds. However, not all of these results offer genuine and credible solutions to those seeking online jobs. As a matter of fact, you shouldn't be surprised to learn that there are countless conmen who are keen on stealing from all those seeking to start making a living out of doing online jobs. This means that you must always be on the lookout so as not to fall into the hands of those conmen.

Even if you're an experienced freelancer, you still have to be very careful so as not to be duped into giving out your cash to these criminals. Some of them work in cartels from different parts of the world and it is therefore quite difficult for them to be caught and prosecuted. Even when caught, they often go scot free due to the fact that it is very difficult for prosecutors to prove any wrong doing on the part of the conmen. This means that it is your responsibility to avoid cyber criminals as much as possible. If they manage to swindle your cash, bully you or steal your identity, there is very little you can do about it. If you are keen on securing your internet presence and avoiding cyber criminals, here are some of the things that you can do:

- Mind your password

The nature of password you select can easily influence whether somebody will take control of your online accounts and therefore steal from you. If you're keen on securing your online business, you have to create very strong passwords for all your accounts. This means that the passwords should have several characters preferably more than ten. The passwords should also not be related to an event in your life including birthdays or anniversaries. It is also good that you avoid commonly used passwords and patterns such as '000000000', '1111111', 'a b c d e f' etc. You must also ensure that your password(s) is a closely guarded secret. Remember that all a fraudster needs is your password and email address and then they can take control of your online activity within a matter of seconds.

- Don't mix your professional and social profiles

One of the biggest mistakes that some people make is using the same email address and password for their professional accounts and accounts in social networking sites. If possible, you should create two unique and independent emails: one for your social networking websites and the other one for professional purposes.

- Change your emails as soon as you detect something fishy

You must never continue using an email if you suspect somebody has accessed it without your authorization. If you ever notice anything unusual, all you'll need to do is change the password or create a new email altogether. As soon as you've changed your email address and/or password, a hacker won't be able to access your accounts.

- Be careful about how you use your credit cards

Credit cards normally contain sensitive personal information that shouldn't be accessed by unauthorized people. This means that you must be very careful when registering in websites that require authentication through credit cards. You can only use your credit cards on secure networks and when creating accounts on reliable networks only.

- Secure your home Wi-Fi network

Unlike other types of internet connections, it is much, much easy to hack into an unsecured Wi-Fi internet connection. This means that the only way you can ensure that your computers at home are not accessed by unauthorized people is by securing the wireless internet connections. Only trusted people should be given the password to your home's Wi-Fi internet connection.

- Log out before closing any webpage when using public computers

Normally, websites store cookies in a browser so that you don't have to keep on logging in every time. Cookies also help store information about your preferences when visiting a particular website. This means that somebody might still be able to see the page you just closed if you didn't logout. You should therefore ensure that you've logged off before closing any page.

- Use of an antivirus and firewall

Apart from helping stop/filter malware and spyware, an antivirus can also help you avoid hackers. When connected to the internet a firewall will help protect your computer from being accessed remotely by somebody else. With this and many more advantages of having an antivirus and firewall, you must always ensure that they're active and updated as frequently as possible.

- Avoid suspicious websites

Before logging into any website, it is always important to ensure that it is a genuine website. There are so many websites impersonating popular websites and hence you should be cautious so as to avoid them as much as possible. Even if the website is genuine, you still have to make sure that the owner(s)/administrators are not after acquiring your private details. So as to gauge a given website's authenticity, all you need to do is search it online and see what other people have to say about it. If the website is run by frauds, you'll probably not be the first person to try and create an account with it. This means that you'll likely to find somebody else who's criticized it on the internet.

Conclusion

Just like any other job, online jobs require a lot of dedication, effort and time. Due to the large physical distance between clients and freelancers, you might be tempted not to take these jobs with the seriousness they deserve. However, if you're keen on being successful with online jobs, you have to be cautious on how you handle the jobs. Now that you've read this book, you know the kind of jobs that you can do over the internet. You also know how you can grow your resume and start making huge sums of money within no time. It is now up to you to go and implement the tips listed in this book.

You also know how to secure your business from cyber criminals anywhere in the world. This means that there is absolutely no reason as to why anybody should take control of your online accounts. You're solely responsible for everything that happens to your online business.

Go ahead and start making unlimited amounts of online cash with the tips listed in this book!!!

Author Bio

Colvin Tonya Nyakundi

Colvin Tonya Nyakundi is a freelance writer and co-author of 'How to Start Making Money Online' Apart from that book, he has a portfolio of several other publications accumulated in the more than two years that he has been freelancing through www.odesk.com.

In addition to his interest in entrepreneurial publications he has authored several personal relationships, lifestyle, travel and holiday guides, and real estate publications. Other books that he has co-authored include 'How to Survive in the Woods', 'How to Survive in a Desert', 'How to Improve Your Communication Skills,' 'Construction Guide for New Investors in Real Estate,' 'How to Make Your Backyard a Magnificent Venue for Hosting Events', 'How to Identify the Perfect Holiday Destination', "How Your Favorite Meal Could be Killing You Slowly" and How to Prepare and Survive in a Foreign Country.' You can get in touch with him through his official Facebook account, tonyanc@facebook.com.

How to Make Money Online

Elda Watulo and John Davidson
JD-Biz Publishing

Entrepreneur Book Series

Disclaimer

The information in this book is provided for informational purposes only and it is not intended for use as a substitute for proper financial or legal direction by a qualified financial or legal advisor. The information is believed to be accurate as presented based on research by the author.

No claims of income are given and examples are used to portray the ideas of the author as possibilities without representing actual earnings that can be made.

The author or publisher is not responsible for financial loss or damage incurred by implementing ideas mentioned in this book. The author or publisher is not responsible for errors or omissions that may exist.

Warning

The Book is for informational purposes only and before starting or running any business, it is recommended that you consult with your financial or legal professional. Always follow all laws and regulations regarding taxes, selling, buying, or ecommerce.

HOW TO MAKE MONEY ONLINE

TABLE OF CONTENTS

INTRODUCTION

Imagine a world without money or any other form of currency. One where everything you need is always at your reach and you do not have to part with anything in order to get it! Everything would be so simple and we would be so happy as stress levels would be reduced by more than seventy per cent. But that's just what it is; an imagination!

Now let's get back to reality! In this world, money is what we call a necessary evil. We simply can't do without it. You can't eat without money. Heck you can't even drink, sleep or wear clothes without money. As such, we need to be always on our toes on learning the quickest and smartest ways of making money.

In this book, we will be looking at the various ways of making money online and the best part is you can do all these in the comfort of your own home.

CHAPTER 1

WHAT INTERNET TRADE ARE YOU INTERESTED IN?

We owe so much to the technological revolution. Thanks to it, the whole world has been turned into a global village. What does this mean? You can be able to buy a Toyota car in Japan whilst in your house in Georgia all with a few clicks of your mouse or you could be a flower vendor in Florida who distributes flowers all over the world after your clients have ordered online. The list of things you can do with the internet is endless. Here we look at the various ways you can engage your internet and mental skills to make a killing, financially.

Virtual Assistant

With the current economy, most employers are looking to cut their operational costs. As such instead of hiring personal assistants and having to part with a lot of cash in the name of buying a computer, office desk and other costs in form of taxes and allowances; they are opting for virtual assistants who they pay on an hourly basis and as per contract. If you possess administrative skills, this is a great niche to venture in. If you play your cards right, you can work for more than one employer. All you need is a computer and good connectivity. At the end of the day, nothing beats working from home!

Create a brand

Many mums prefer staying home to raise their kids. Let's face it; no person is going to nurture a kid better than its mother. However, more often than not, this usually leaves the man of the house with a very huge financial burden. From experience, I can honestly say that stay at home mums are the most innovative, they come up with very unique business ideas. If you are such a mum, take advantage of the internet and create a brand from your idea. Run the idea past your friends and gauge their reaction. If you get more than eighty per cent positive feedback, then you know that you are onto something. Go to the internet and start advertising yourself and in the process, you will get noticed by someone interested in your product and before you know it, you will be smiling all the way to the bank.

Blog! Blog! Blog!

Blogging is the new way to make cash. Over seventy per cent of bloggers don't know that their material is worth thousands of dollars. Most people do it for fun and are not really keen on making cash out of it. But what better way of making money is there than through doing what you love most? You can even do guest blogs for established websites and products and get paid per blog posting. Another way is to create a website and gather a huge following on the internet by posting really interesting and informative stuff. With time you can make use of things like getting paid per click made on your website.

Freelancing

You can stick to your profession and make huge sums of money. If you are a writer, an accountant, web developer, actuary, I could go on and on; there a number of websites such as elance, odesk, academia and what have you that pair up freelancers and clients who want some job done for them. You get paid for every complete job and both you and the client are given an opportunity to rate each other. The higher your rating, the better jobs you get.

Social media marketing

This is all the rage right now. Facebook, LinkedIn, twitter, fiverr.com and any other social media out there is the best way to sell your product. The first step is to woo viewers to follow you on these media and get them to like your product(s). After that, you will now rely on your followers to pass the word to their friends and their friends to their friends' friends' and so on and so forth. Word on social media literally spreads like bush fire. The most important thing is to remain relevant and consistent, remember a single mistake has the potential to be your downfall as the word will spread. You will be surprised at how much faster a bad word will spread compared to a good word.

Seminars and tutorials

A teaching program is another really fast way of making money online. The internet is evolving faster than ever before and it is a wonder that we are sometimes able to keep up. There are so many new programs popping up every single day and you could take advantage of this. Stay updated on anything that relates to the internet and technology. You can create online seminars and tutorials where you teach people on the new ways of doing things on the internet. This way you will help other people learn a lot about the internet while you get richer by the minute.

Sell your talent

Are you an amazing singer, actor or any other kind of entertainer but do not have the money to go to a talent manager or a recording company? Worry not; the internet has got you covered. With platforms like YouTube, you can take a brief recording of you doing your thing and then upload it on YouTube. Within a couple of minutes or hours, you will have received a lot of hits if you are really good. Nowadays, talent managers are not relying on the old school method of holding auditions in order to discover talent like they did in the past. They go to the most viewed videos in YouTube ad get the talent they are looking for.

There are so many things you could do on the internet but these are the main ones. If you know of other trades you can explore, please feel free, do not feel restricted at all.

CHAPTER 2

WHAT DOES YOUR WEBSITE SAY ABOUT YOU?

Usually, when you see someone for the first time, you gauge them by their appearance. Especially for a blind date, you practically know nada about the person you are meeting and all you have to judge them is their look. A sharply dressed individual will score higher than one who seemed to have grabbed the nearest outfit. So it is with your website. What is the first impression you get when you visit your website. What I my thinking? You will most likely give me a biased answer. You can ask one of your closest friends who you know will be one hundred per cent honest with you.

You definitely don't want people visiting your website and going like, "Oh my, what was he/she thinking?" There are things to consider

when creating a website. If you want to generate a lot of business, please adhere to these and you will never look back.

Aesthetic appeal

Your website should be like an exquisite flower, tastefully done. One look at your website should inspire a number of clicks to learn more on what the website is really about. Make it bright but don't use all the colours of the rainbow such as the effect is confusion. Seek the help of a web designer if you feel this is beyond your scope and communicate your vision and let them do the bulk of the work for you. Ensure your website is as beautiful as possible and this way you will attract lots of followers as they too will acknowledge the work that went into creating your website.

What is your clientele?

One common mistake many websites make is to oversell their brand. They rave on and on about how great they are but forget completely who it is they want to sell their product to. Your business should be wholly cantered around your customers. They need to feel involved and appreciated and as such, your website should fully convey this message. Identify your clientele and tell them exactly what is in it for them. By doing this, you will have spiked some interest on their part and they will want to know more about your website.

Go straight to the point

There is nothing as annoying as someone beating about the bush instead of saving you both some time and telling you exactly what they want. Apply this to your website and you will have many happy followers. Stay true to the message of your website. Aim to be informative in a creative and engaging way whilst remaining relevant. Do not use a thousand words when a hundred words would have sufficed!

Be interactive

The best way to maintain a happy following is to create a platform where your viewers can air their views openly without feeling intimidated. You can do this by writing blogs and inviting your audience to comment or write their own views. But remember, you will never get a hundred per cent positive views; there are a number of haters out there whose job is to trample on other peoples' feelings. When responding to such comments, don't let your anger get the better of you, instead use some humour in humiliating them. For the positive comments or constructive criticisms; respond promptly by thanking them and telling them that you have put their views under consideration.

When clients feel like they are part of your brand, they will grow more and more loyal to you and even inspire potential clients to join your following.

Stay updated

The internet is continually evolving on a daily basis and so should your website. Always remain relevant by updating your site on a daily basis if possible. It is 2014; you should not be having 2012 December as the date of your most recent blog. This will make your audience start questioning your legitimacy.

SEO

Search Engine Optimization is one concept that every website owner worth their salt makes use of. You do not have to make payments for your website to rank at the very top when anyone searches on Google for example. If you continually update your website then your site will rise to the very top every time a person searches something close to what you deal in or exactly what you deal in.

These are the basic steps that will ensure your website is a success. This is the first step in making money online especially if you are selling a brand or product. We are slowly moving towards exclusive online shopping. Be on the right track with these simple guidelines.

CHAPTER 3

SOCIAL MEDIA

Research has shown that the number of people using their phones to access social media is at its all-time high since the inception of social media and smart phones. To top it all, the number of people above 45 years of age who have joined the social media is above 30% of all social media users. This makes it the best platform to advertise your brand, product or campaign.

Social media has also evolved to the point where you can use it for equity and debt raising as well as financing. This is an awesome thing as it holds the potential to take your business to the next level in terms of getting financed by venture capitalists as well as other big shots interested in your campaign. The main aim is to put yourself out there in the best light so that you convey the right message about your product.

You can turn social media into your personal cash cow. However, you need to adhere to these three simple rules.

Be adventurous

Do not stick to only one form of social media such as Facebook only, instead use at least three or four platforms and link them together. It is possible to link twitter with Facebook, linked in and what have you. This way every update you make on one platform will be reflected on all the other platforms and you will therefore end up reaching a larger multitude of followers.

Aim at creating a community

Social media is not all about writing posts after posts after posts. No, it is about interaction. Create your own community where your viewers can openly respond to your posts by commenting and liking your posts and pages. Acknowledge all activity from them and make them feel appreciated and part of your team.

Sustain your campaign

Do not just send out one message and stop at that. Social media is now the main media of letting the word out to the masses. As such you need to continually post on social media and creating a buzz around your campaign so that as many people as possible get to learn more about your campaign.

Social media is the cheapest way to get the word out about your campaign or brand. You cannot compare it to advertising on TV in terms of cost but the outcome in most cases is better than advertising on TV.

Again, advertising on social media is not restrictive at all. If you see something that would be useful to your campaign, go ahead and copy it. Get some pointers from other people in the same line of business as you. Steal what works for you. You don't have to use a lot of time and energy reinventing the wheel!

Use your friends to help spread the word as well as liking other popular pages that are in line with your brand or campaign, this way, you will be able to attract those who like these pages to also like yours.

If you are starting out, invite social media users to join your campaign; choose a creative and magnetic name for your campaign or brand and enlist the help of other people to help promote your page(s). Remember the reason you are successful on social media is because of your followers. Stay faithful to them and interact with them at least twice a week or every single day if you have the time by posting trending topics and seeking for their feedback.

Don't be left behind, stay on the bandwagon by using this amazing platform to smile all the way to the bank by promoting your brand and staying current in the best platform yet to let the word out!

CHAPTER 4

JACK OF ALL TRADES

If your aim is to make considerable amounts of cash online, you have no choice but to be a jack of all trades. Do a number of small gigs and before you know it these small streams will eventually become a huge flowing river of cash. There are so many opportunities online that have not been fully explored.

Create an all- in- one website

Yeah, I know you are a bit confused by this term but what I mean is; create a website that comprises of all the services that you offer indicating the price and delivery time. As we had talked about earlier on, create an authentic website that meets all the requirements we had spoken about. So if you are a freelancer who also does flower deliveries, be sure to include these services in your website.

Writing services

Start up a writing service that caters to content creation, ghost writing, writing business plans, guest blogs and any other thing you can think of. The best way to do this is to create a company of writers that comprises of writers with different writing skills. Register your company with a platform like Elance and Odesk and start applying for writing jobs. When done in the right way, that is creating unique content free of plagiarism, this has the potential to turn into a very solid money making venture.

Conduct surveys

There are so many companies, institutions as well as individuals who want to carry out surveys but do not have the time and the resources required such as the sample population. The internet has changed the way surveys used to be done. Now, you can get a ready sample online and the best part is that you can readily get a sample population based on the topic you are researching. So many people still haven't discovered this and you can make hay while it still shines by venturing into this business. Carry out surveys on other peoples' behalf and you will be happy with the results.

Disseminate answers

Gone are the days when you went back to the manufacturer to tell them that you couldn't assemble the cupboard or coffee machine you bought from them or even went to the doctor for every minor ache. We have a pool of experts online ready to answer questions on virtually everything. Do you consider yourself a brainy or info junkie? If so, this is your sort of gig. If you are a person who likes to read on different topics then you can affiliate yourself with sites such as JustAnswer.com and share your knowledge. This is turning into a booming business with an ever rising number of people who ask questions on nearly all topics on the internet. The 'how to' guides is where the money is so you can focus on them.

Venture into online auctioning

Most people, including you, have so much stuff in their houses that they don't use. This ends up cramping the house with stuff that one doesn't really need. You can take advantage of this niche and start auctioning stuff on the net in websites like eBay and Amazon. To start with, create a seller's profile and start by selling your own stuff. Spread your wings by offering this service to your friends and then later on you can advertise yourself on social media and you can make money by selling off other people's stuff. Another way of doing this is carrying out an actual trade where you buy things that you have noticed to sell easily on eBay or any other auction site and then reselling them at a profit. Before you know it you will be enjoying steady streams of profit!

Engage your creative art abilities

If you consider yourself a decent artist then you can really make some decent money online. Whether you are a clothes designer or a portrait artist, there is always a way for you to make cash. Start off small by maybe showing some of your best design jobs by posting pictures of your creations; you can also post portraits you have done next to the actual pictures of the people who you drew. This way you will get audiences to really appreciate your raw talent. Make it a constant thing, do not just post one thing then go all for the next two months. Be consistent and you are sure to gather a number of clients.

Purchase and resale of domain names

You are familiar with the business of buying dead beat houses, refurbishing them and selling them at a higher price. This is the same principle you are going to apply here. If you search on the internet on virtually anything, there are some websites that come up that are quite obsolete, that is, you find some which were last updated two years ago. What you do is buy their domain names, they mostly go for a few hundred dollars (go for the really dead beat one's for you to get the lowest price.) now, do a complete overhaul by making use of the points we spoke about creating a successful website. After all your hard work, you can be sure to make even ten times what the site was worth. With the internet, it's all about being smart and identifying your niche.

Hand-made products

There is nothing as exquisite and unique as a well-made handmade product. Be it a pot, a hand bag, necklace, bracelet or anything you can think of. People tend to appreciate the work that goes into handmade products compared to what's made by machines. This is a great niche to explore. You do not have to be the creator; you can be the middle man by finding someone who crafts handmade objects and help sell their wares online. EBay and Amazon are great websites for this kind of thing. I know what you are thinking. Are they not auctioning sites? Well, they are not just limited to auction products; they can also be used to sell original things. Focus on your passion and you will be inspired to do marvellous things!

CHAPTER 5

WHO IS YOUR MENTOR?

The reason why so many people do not make it in life is because they do not have someone they can look up to. You probably don't think that a mentor is a great asset. If so, am afraid to say that you are absolutely wrong. There are so many great people you can look up to and copy their recipe for success. For example, who knew Mark Zuckerbug would be one of the richest men in the world all because he had a vision and a passion that he followed. These are the kind of people to look up to.

In life, we all need something to believe in and this thing is what motivates us to be the best we can be and follow our dreams and eventually become successful in all sectors of our lives. If you are to succeed, you need that one person who is in the same line of business as you or in the same field as you who has managed to achieve great levels of success, to look up to and to copy what he did so you can also attain similar levels of success if not more.

If I put my guessing power to use, the top question on your mind is, "How do I get a mentor online?" there are actually a number of things you should consider before settling down for a certain individual:

What are you looking for?

Make a list of qualities that a person must meet to be your mentor. Don't be too specific but also do not be too vague. One important quality should be that your mentor should be in your field and should be higher than you in the hierarchy. This is not necessarily for a company setting. Your mentor should have more experience than you and should have a proven track record. This is very important if you are aiming to follow in the same path as your mentor will be your guide towards making your dream a reality.

Expand your horizon

Do not limit yourself to finding your mentor in your online company. No, you can expand your search to online mentorship programs that pair you with the person who best suits your line of work. They also take into consideration the qualities you are looking for. Remember, you are looking for an online mentor so you could be in Canada but end up having a mentor in Australia. What is important is that you get a mentor who inspires you to succeed and overcome all challenges. There are many mentorship programs on the internet so get clicking and add someone special to your life.

Be a great student

Once you have gotten your mentor, do not treat him/her like your peer even though he/she may be. Be respectful under all circumstances and always keep time when meeting with your mentor. A good student goes to class with a notebook and pen. Carry this for every meeting as you are sure to learn something new. Do not be coy about asking questions. This is your great opportunity to learn something new that is going to take you, your brand or product to the next level. Inspire your mentor to teach you all he/she knows by being the best student ever!

Thank you goes a long way

Your mentor is a person with a busy schedule who has slotted you into his program. Remember to show a lot of gratitude for the time he/she has set apart for you. You can do this by word of mouth or make it more special by sending him/her a thank you note. Either way, let it be known that you do not take the time you spend together for granted.

Market yourself

Why should the person you would like to mentor you accept to do so? Be sure anyone you approach to mentor you will ask themselves this question. You should create a sort of sales pitch that is not too corny but that portrays you in the best light. Remember, your mentor-to-be is a busy person and one who surrounds him/herself with successful people. Market yourself as a rocket ready to launch. Do not be modest; instead, be sure to portray a lot of potential.

Younger mentor

Senior citizens who are fifty years and above should have younger mentors! This is because the world is operating differently from their eras. With technology, everything is now different. An older person will need to be coached on the new ways of doing things whilst still offering advice on things that they are good at.

Drop formality

Drop the old school kind of looking for a mentor for instance, "I am so and so, kindly be my mentor." I assure you with this approach online you are not going to get any mentor worth his/ her salt! This sounds so tiring and like you are asking someone to do your house chores for you! Move with the digital world and bring some Zen in asking someone to be your mentor. You want to show your potential mentor that you know exactly what you are doing so you can start by asking for a piece of advice on something in your line of business that you know he is familiar with. This way he will be motivated to take you under his/her wing.

Mentor someone

Listen first, do not put yourself down even though you are just starting out. This will go a very long way in teaching you how to communicate with your mentor. To start with, enrol in volunteer programs or your church where you speak to kids about following their dreams and the importance of always maintaining a positive attitude and answering all their questions. This will give you a deeper insight on what your relationship with your mentor should be like.

CHAPTER 6

SUCCESS LIES IN YOUR ATTITUDE

The way you have programmed your brain to operate is what is going to dictate success or failure in your life. As from 'the secret,' a positive attitude is all you need to be successful in life. So you want to make money online, what is your current mind-set? You must have sat down and calculated your income and seen that you need to do something extra or do something differently. Just because you have not yet secured employment or have been recently fired doesn't mean that you are a failure. The first rule of thumb is to believe in yourself and believe that whatever you put your hands on is going to succeed.

Look at the founder of Facebook, Mark Zuckerbug, who knew the dream in his head was going to make him a super-rich man at his age. Of course there were people who laughed at his dream but where are they now? Do not let negative people put you down. For as long as you know what you want in life and have laid out a plan, go ahead and live your dream. Not be cliché but 'if it can be dreamt, it can be lived'

Surround yourself with positive energy and your success will know no boundaries. Believe in yourself and your project and you will be the most successful person online. This is how you make money online: a positive attitude and lots of work and dedication to fulfil your plan. No more slacking or sleeping till noon. It is time to make a few tweaks in your life

Read the stories of the most successful people in the world and ask yourself what they all have in common. I will tell you the first thing; a positive attitude. Do not underestimate the power of your word and mind set. A little faith will go a long way in making you a force to reckon with.

Take a pen and paper and write down why you are an awesome person and that you believe whatever you are going to put your hands on is going to blossom into the most beautiful flower of success. Every time you feel a bit low, go through this and reignite the fire within you that is looking to succeed!

TIME TO SAY ADIEU!

All through the book we have looked at ways to help you make money online. As with any business, you are bound to hit a few pot holes but if you stay resilient and continue working hard you are going to experience success in a way you never thought possible.

Stay positive and continue researching on whatever line of business you are in so that you are not left behind every time there are new inventions and innovations in the internet. All the best and let this be your go to guide. Do not read it once; go through it time after time to ensure that you internalise everything and I guarantee you are going to make so much money online if you follow these simple guidelines!

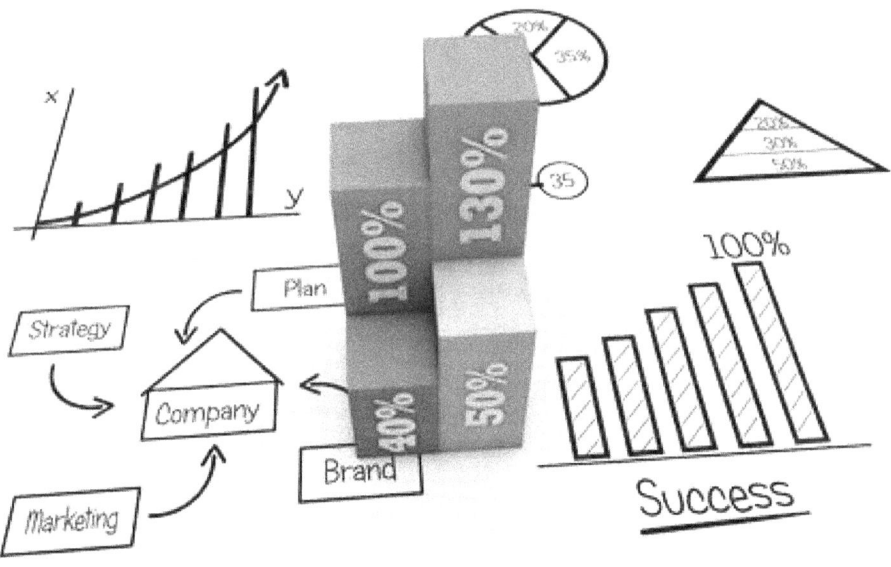

Good luck! May success follow you into the future.

Author Bio

Elda Watulo is a Canada-based author of many award-winning books on different topics. She has published several health/fitness, business and marketing books and she blogs at Hubpages.com.

Check out some of the other JD-Biz Publishing books

Gardening Series on Amazon

Health Learning Series

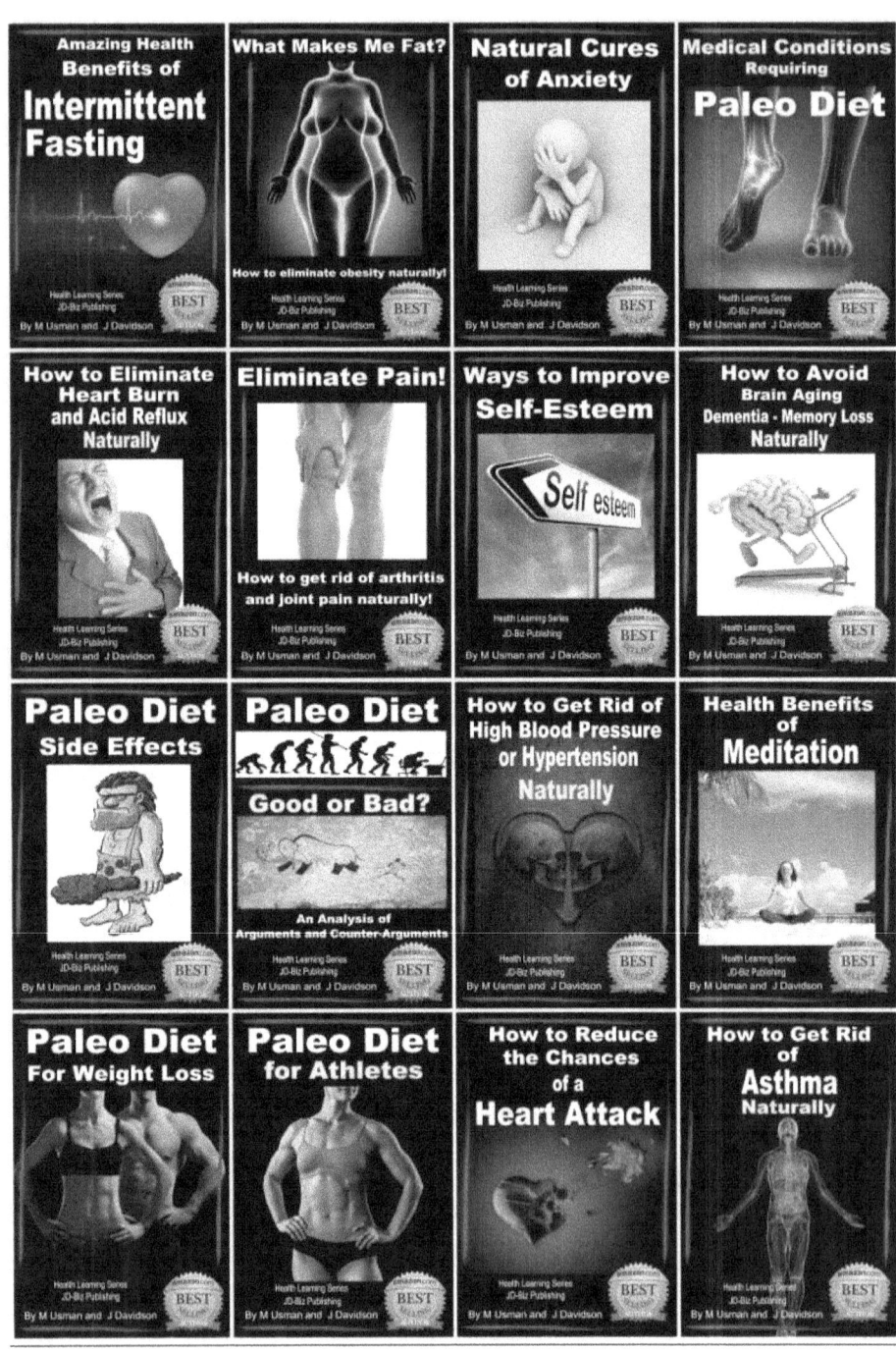

Amazing Animal Book Series

Learn To Draw Series

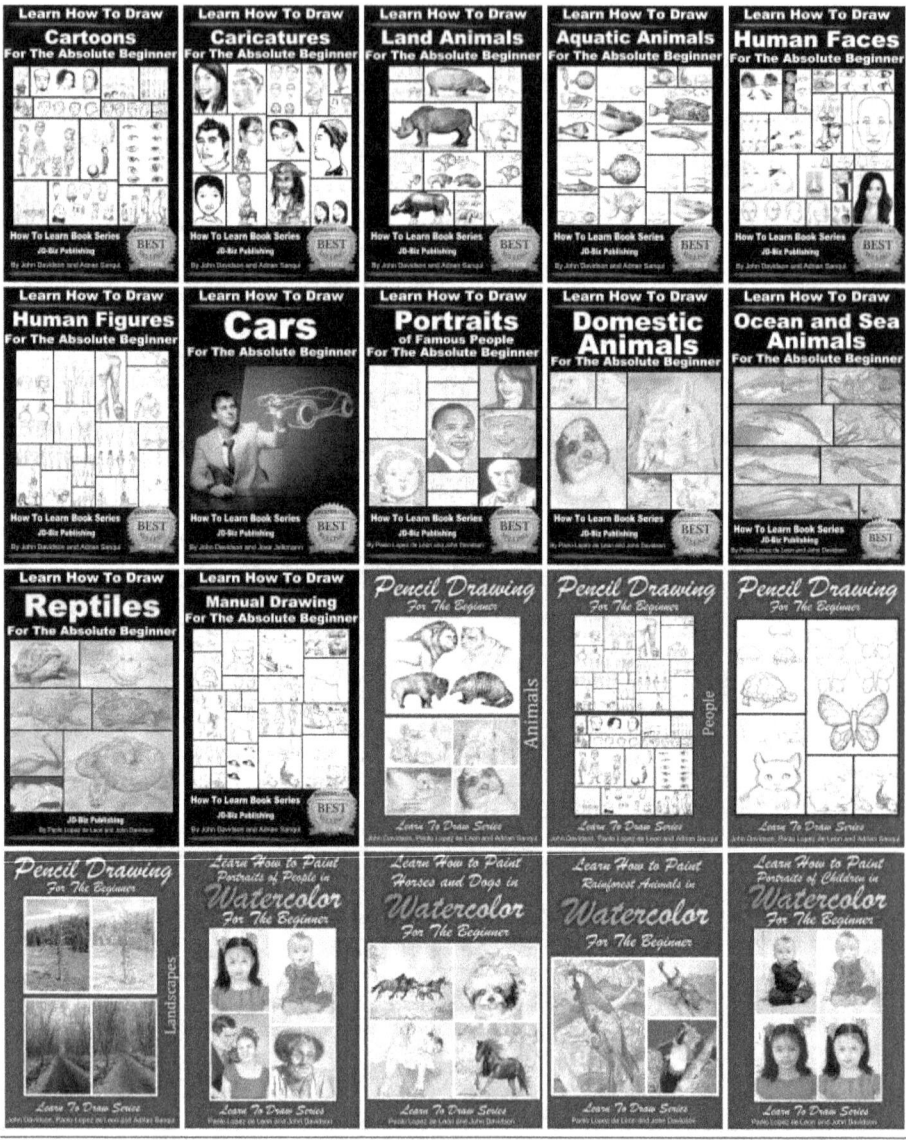

How to Build and Plan Books

Entrepreneur Book Series

Our books are available at

1. Amazon.com

2. Barnes and Noble

3. Itunes

4. Kobo

5. Smashwords

6. Google Play Books

Puiblisher

JD-Biz Corp

P O Box 374

Mendon, Utah 84325

http://www.jd-biz.com/

Mendon Cottage Books

P O Box 374, Mendon Utah 84325

www.ingramcontent.com/pod-product-compliance
Lightning Source LLC
Chambersburg PA
CBHW072309200526
45168CB00014B/1167